Heart on a Platter

Rhianna Parra-Hughes

BookLeaf Publishing

Presentation by *BookLeaf Publishing*

Web: www.bookleafpub.com

E-mail: info@bookleafpub.com

ISBN: 9789357618755

First edition 2022

DEDICATION

To my wife, for always believing in my dreams.

To my son, for always having patience with me.

To my daughter, for changing my heart and being my greatest gift.

Ugly

I'd like to write beautiful things, but
I'm afraid I don't have beautiful things to say.

Sweet Teeth and Broken Hearts

As I child my heart was broken by
A baker who told me that wheat pennies
Couldn't be baked into a loaf of bread,
And that they weren't even worth much to begin with.

I was one who always tried to see the value
In everything from politics to casserole, and I have always
Had a sweet tooth, so when I saw you I knew I needed
To save up a bushel of wheat pennies for a taste of your sugar.

Our fates were once intertwined like a fat child's
Fingers and the sticks of a dozen lollipops.
But sooner or later sugar forms cavities,
And there is no dentist for love.

And I realized the baker was right after all.

Silver Lining

Cheer up, little flower. I know the sun isn't shining, but
Your roots are a bit deeper in the ground than you think.
If I could, I would paint rainbows over your gloomy skies
And sprinkle raindrops over your fading petals.
I know the clouds must have a silver lining because
I see the lining of hope around your heart.

Newspaper Feelings

You will never know how I feel about you.
I will never tell you.
I want to hug you, hold you, kiss you.
But I don't, I won't, I never will.

Sometimes there's this glimmer in your eyes.
You smile, and the corners of your lips turn up
ever so slightly.
And then your eyes laugh at me. They laugh at
me, and
Then you turn away, focusing again on whatever
you were doing before.
You get this look sometimes and I can't help but
wonder what it means.
What does it mean?
Good God, what does it mean?!?!
No, no, it doesn't mean what I think it means.
Forget it. Don't think about it.
Be cool, stay calm.
Cross your arms, cross your legs, cross your
heart.
Cross everything worth crossing.

You will never know how I feel about you.
I will never tell you.

You will never like me, want me, love me.
You don't, you won't, you never will.

My feelings for you are like a newspaper.
I take out my feelings, read them, can't bear to
look at them.
So I dump them in this week's recycling.
Get out of here, you shouldn't be here, I can't
think about you anymore.
Then the next morning when I wake up,
My feelings for you are sitting on the porch
Waiting to be read.

Fuck.

Seaweed

Your eyes remind me of seaweed,
Entrancing me as I feel you snake around me
and pull me down.
Your love is the ocean, and I am sinking fast.
Drowning in your tangled seaweed eyes,
Your salt stings my heart like a million electric
eels.
I hit rock bottom with a jolt and schools of neon
fish
Swim around me like each colorful memory of
you swims in my head.
My heart has died a strange death, where I am
Wrapped in your seaweed, bound to your deep
blue love
Where I will stay engulfed forever.

Fox on Fire

I don't know how to get out of this trap.
I'm a fox buried in my burrow, and I'm trying to stay
nestled, warm in my bed where I know that I'm safe.
I know that I'm accepted here; I know I'm supposed
to be here. This is my home. What reason would I
have to leave?

But then you happened.

You're the hunter's fire that is licking at the sides of
my hole. Your smoke is billowing down my tunnel,
and I'm choking. You're engulfing me in flames and
I'm burning. Burning alive. There's no hope for me
now.
My only choice is to claw myself out of the other end
of my burrow. But those woods out there…those are
unchartered woods. I've never been out there.

I'm scared.

I can't leave my burrow. I know that I'm expected
here. This is my home; this is where I'm loved. And
with this soot in my eyes, I'd be chartering the
unknown blindly.

All I know is that if I step outside these walls, there's
no turning back.

Mincemeat Heart

I can't decide if this is the happiest I've been in
years
Or the most scared.
I've never been good at this whole vulnerability
thing,
And here my heart has been put on a platter and
served
As the main course.

It's a fancy occasion, this feast called life.
A black tie event, I suppose.
Tablecloths, chandeliers, fine china
And the best wine your pocketbook can afford.
The glasses begin clinking as a signal for the
meal to start.
Your platter comes to the table; the silver dome
is lifted off
And you inspect my heart on your platter.
I feel meager, small. I am most definitely not
the juiciest cut or
The meatiest tenderloin at this feast.
I have greasy edges, fatty spots, and burnt
corners.
I know that I'm far from perfect, but I also know
that I have

Flavor hidden inside somewhere.
Yet you continue to examine my heart on your
platter
With your fork held in the air, mouth salivating.
I lay exposed, eagerly awaiting for you to take a
chance;
To just try a piece, or maybe even devour the
entire course.

Some days when I'm with you, I feel like
The luckiest girl in the world.
But others, I can't help but curse
At myself in the mirror and wonder
Why I can't be good enough for you.

The Trick Glass

You are a glass.
Intricate, shining, lots of details and designs spun up
to make your edges.
One of a kind, I found you in a pawn shop.
I wasn't really looking for anything. I was just kind
of browsing one day
When a glimmer of light hit my retinas, washed over
them like rainbows.
I squinted to find the source of the mini disco balls
dancing across my shirt
When I saw you.
The moment I saw you, I knew I needed to have you.
It's funny, I thought. I have plenty of other glasses at
home.
I didn't really need you. You were an oddball, a
mismatch, alone on the shelf.
But you were different and beautiful and I just
couldn't pass you up.
It's hard to set something back down that reminds you
what the colors of the rainbow look like.
Something that reminds you what true colors really
are, what they mean.
So I snatched you up. You were a steal, really.
It's a wonder no one figured it out before me.
But when I got you home I figured out your mystery.

You are a trick glass.

Sometimes I fill you up to the brim and the liquid sits
inside.
Glistening like I poured in fine jewels instead of
water.
But other times when I turn my back, those designs
spun around your edges
Spew the water in a hundred directions.
Little holes spit the water across the floor
And I run around with dozens of styrofoam cups
To try to catch all of the water like buckets under a
leaky roof.
But I just don't understand why
You let the water go to waste and why
You like to make a mess of my floor.
I don't like these tricks.
Sometimes I get frustrated, and I think of knocking
you off the counter
Where you'd shatter into a billion bits on the ceramic
floor.

But ah, I wouldn't do that.
I still put up with you.
I have plenty of other glasses, remember?
But none that make the disco balls dance around
The way that you do.

Rooster

You are the sun, and I am a rooster. And if the
sun stopped rising, the rooster
would never want to sing again. And you know
that roosters love singing, right?
It's their passion. They don't have much else to
live for. But without the sun,
they don't even care.
And without the sun, the world goes silent
without their songs.
The world goes silent without their songs.
The world goes silent.
Silent.

...

Empty

Your fingertips trace cookie cutters over my heart
Taking all that mattered and leaving only an imprint.

Please

There are butterflies in my stomach, and
They are finally fluttering again instead of
Kicking me in the spleen,
Which is what they had been doing for the last couple
of months or so.

It used to feel like cheese graters were slicing through
my stomach, and
Although my stomach doesn't feel torn to pieces
anymore,
My stomach is still churning.
Luckily this time I like the reason my stomach isn't
cooperating very well.

You think I'm shy and that it's cute, which is
something I don't usually hear.
Most people would like it if I'd shut up for a while.
When I actually am quiet, most people assume I'm
considering jumping off a bridge or something.
I don't usually hear that it's cute.

You poke me and tickle me which drives me a bit
crazy.
It's definitely not my favorite thing in the world, but I
take it in stride because
I like the feel of your hands on me even if it seems
like torture.
Hopefully that doesn't make me sound crazy.

There was one night in particular that you set gentle
fingertips on my leg and
I suddenly felt a shock zip up my body and spread
heat from
The top of my head to the soles of my feet.
Is it normal for me to be affected so strongly by you?

You ask me why I'm so quiet around you sometimes,
and I shrug, saying I don't really know.
That I like when you talk, sometimes I
don't have things to say, and maybe I'm just shy
because I like you and I don't want you to change
your mind about me.

But really I'm afraid that if I talked more, I would say
things that I don't want escaping my lips:
I want you.
Just take me and hold me close.
Please don't go.
Please don't break my heart.
There's something about you, and I don't know what
it is.
I can't quite put my finger on it.

Piranha

We all have old skeletons in our closets. Past memories that hide in the darkness in boxes and binders and photographs.
But one of your skeletons isn't really a skeleton at all. She is living, breathing, out in the sunlight. She laughs, she cries, she thinks, she feels.

And I find myself wishing she really was a skeleton.

Because I see her. And I think of you. I think of you tracing her cheek with your thumb. I see you kissing her and tucking her hair behind her ears. I hear you whispering to her about how much you love her. I think of you laying beside her and holding her in your arms. I hear you laughing with her and telling each other secrets.
I see you staring into her eyes and wanting her.
I think of you wanting nothing else but her.
And that kills me.
Who does she think she is, having a place in your heart? And sure, maybe she was there first.
But I'm there now, and I want her to stay out.
But I'm so afraid that she will try to find a way

back in. I'm afraid she will wave a magic wand
and you will walk back to her in some sort of
trance. But I know she's no magician. I can see
through the "pull the rabbit out of the hat" act. I
know what she really is.
She's some sort of virus. Some sort of poison
that makes me fear you will want her instead.
Some sort of venom that makes me fear you will
let her enter your heart again. Some sort of
beast that makes me fear that my love isn't good
enough.
She is a piranha in my swimming pool. I know
she shouldn't be in there, and yet she eats away
at me anyways.

Judge Me

Why do you give up on me so easily?
I am still the same person.
Sure, I have changed
But I'm not completely different.

I would still hitchhike across the country
If you needed me.
I would still bust a sorry ass
If someone broke your heart.
I would still do your dirty work for you
If you wanted my help.
And my shoulder would still be ready
If you needed a place to cry.

My feelings for you haven't changed,
Even if a few of my choices have.
But those have nothing to do with you.
You can't make my decisions for me.

Sometimes life takes its toll.
I am a tree bent by the wind,
But I am still standing.
Yet you act like I've been chopped down.

I don't want things to be different,
But if you can't see past my faults
And you begin untangling yourself from my
branches,
Well then, I guess I have no choice in the matter.

I won't change who I am,
For you or anyone else.
If you're ready to leave the shade of my bough,
Don't let my tattered vines hit you on your way
out.

Seasons

Just like seasons, people change.
I guess I was naive enough to think that you
Would never be one of those people.
Not to change in small, inevitable ways,
But in the way that you have all but disappeared
From my life. The way that you have gone from
Living on my speed dial, to being one of the
Last people I would call.

Perhaps you are summer
One who has dried out from the heat of a hard season,
Scorched from crimson memories of a past you'd like
to forget.
Am I who you'd like to forget?
A thousand memories of the laughter we shared tells
me otherwise,
But I can't think of another reason for your absence.

Perhaps you are autumn
One who has changed their colors and shed the dead
leaves of the past.
You always liked trees, but maybe you can't stand to
be bare
And are hiding your transformation from peering
eyes.
Am I who you are hiding from?
Shared stories and tears of our past tell me otherwise,

But I can't think of another reason for your
detachment.

Perhaps you are winter
One who has become bitter and cold to those around
you
Piles of snow building around your dreams of the
past
Frozen in time, ashamed of a stagnant position.
Am I who you are ashamed to face?
Memories of shared space, meals, and talks into the
night tell me otherwise
But I can't think of another reason for your
indifference.

Perhaps you are spring
One who has grown into someone new,
unrecognizable.
Washed clean with the showers of a new morning,
A fresh beauty ready to be shared with the world.
Am I not worthy of your metamorphosis?
Our past being wound together so tightly tells me
otherwise,
But I can't think of another reason for your disregard.

Just like seasons, people change.
I guess I was naive enough to think that
Time and distance wouldn't affect what we had.
Perhaps it is me who has changed.
Has one of us changed so much that it has skewed
our alliance?

What happened to devotion? What happened to
loyalty?
What happened to the promises shared and integrities
spoken?
Every time I have reached out, I've been met with
empty words
Or silence stretching across the growing months and
years.
Perhaps I will never have closure
Instead just a fleeting image of a tree
Changing and growing evermore distant.

Narcissist

Are you so determined to create
A new-and-improved version of yourself
That you are satisfied with destroying
Everything he is meant to be?

Cancer

I come into your haven, unwelcomed and feared
Your first action is to shoo me out the door before I
can even take
My shoes off or hang my coat on the hook.
But I am persistent, and I will stay as long as I please
Or until others force me to leave your dwelling.

I have but one job, while you have many.
You wake up, deal with customers, manage
households, read
the newspaper, and order Chinese food.
And yet you seek to end my only profession.
I have come to attack, multiply, and destroy.
I have your organs under siege, your nightmares
under invasion.
I seek your calamity.
You seek my departure.

Like two roosters in a cockfight, we peck
At each other, trying to get our jobs done.
May the one with the sharpest beak win.

Three

Three years is a lifetime when you think of every
detail that has occurred.
Three years is a moment when you think of only one.

Back in my memories of long ago
You were more than just a holograph swimming
before my eyes.
You were right beside me, tangible, I could reach out
and touch
The soft cotton of your shirt, or the stones in your
jewelry.

If I close my eyes tightly I can still smell
Your sweet perfume and see
The gold flecks in your sea-blue eyes, and I can run
My fingers through your dark, bouncy
Curls and nuzzle in your comforting embrace.

If absence makes the heart grow fonder, then my
heart
Is bursting with blistering love. Streaks of
adoration are streaming down the walls of my
memories.

Three years could be three centuries or three hours
when
Absence is scorching your yearning heart.

Inches

I want to be close to you,
But I don't know how.
I scoot two inches closer,
And when I look up
You are two feet away.
Tell me how I can
Make up the distance.
How do I get up to your level
When my anchor has me sinking?
You are light, spreading
Across each room you touch.
I am shadows, inching closer
But never quite reaching you.

Less Than Forever

I may less than three you <3,
but I will never less than four you <4,
because I will never love you less than 4 ever.

Periodically

I know I don't tell you this enough,
That I only periodically express your significance.
In reality, I should be singing of your worthiness
Every hour of every day.
There is never a moment that you are not on my
mind,
I only hope that you know your importance.
You light up my life, like a [Ne] sign in the night,
Pointing weary travelers in the right direction.
My love for you only grows, rising like the [He]
In a thousand balloons headed for the heavens.
You are my constant, stronger than [Ti]
Worth more to me than all the [Ag] and [Au] in the
world
I can never have enough of you, like the [Fe] in my
blood
It seems I always have a deficiency.
I pray I am never lacking your smile or laughter
Or the [Na] our bodies create as we crash together.
An absence from you burns my soul,
The same way [Cl] stings a swimmer's eyes.
I need you the same way I need [O]
Without you, I cannot survive.

The Greatest Gift

I hold your little hand in mine
Sleep in our eyes, milk on your breath
Smiles on our lips, tears on my cheek

Such happiness and sadness all at once
A gift with an unexpected wrapping
A love so strong it hurts, pierces the soul

Overwhelming pride that you are mine
Overwhelming gratitude that I am yours
Overwhelming fear for your well-being

Worrying for seemingly no reason
I wake throughout the night
Just to check for the rise and fall of your chest

Your welfare is now paramount
My own importance pales in comparison
My wishes revolving around your happiness

I wish I could freeze each moment
Already I feel that little details are slipping,
Falling into a distant memory not easily recalled

The grunts of displeasure you make in your sleep
The smooth, untouched skin on the soles of your feet
The flecks in your eyes that change colors each day

The gummy smile that lights up the room
The laughs and cries that punctuate your dreams
The pouty-faced stretches that accompany your
waking

I breathe you in, not wanting to forget
Even the slightest thing about you
Or the smallest thing you've done

I have so many plans for you, for us
Adventures to go on, traditions to follow
Little steps on a path to fill your heart with joy

You my darling, are perfection
A light in the darkest of nights
A giggle in the midst of silent sorrow

You filled an emptiness in my heart
Yet I can only pray to be good enough
To fill your vacant spots as well,
And to never leave a void.